IMAGES
of America

JOHNSONBURG

Life in Johnsonburg is never far from the mill. This is a scene from Johnsonburg Memorial Stadium where the Johnsonburg Rams uphold the pride of the hardworking and hard-playing residents of the town. Loyalty to the blue and gold of the Rams is fierce, and whenever the home 11 conquers the other county schools, it is time to celebrate in the "Paper City." (Author's collection.)

On the cover: The Nypen Club Community Building and playground are shown on Market Street in Johnsonburg at its grand opening. On the right is the Brick Block section of Market Street and, on the left, a portion of the Johnsonburg paper mill. When the mill was known as the New York and Pennsylvania Company, it built this community center. The building housed the Johnsonburg borough offices, public library, gymnasium, and a swimming pool. (Mark Wendel.)

IMAGES
of America

JOHNSONBURG

Dennis McGeehan

ARCADIA
PUBLISHING

Published by Arcadia Publishing
Charleston SC, Chicago IL, Portsmouth NH, San Francisco CA

Library of Congress Control Number: 2009924688

For all general information contact Arcadia Publishing at:
Telephone 843-853-2070
Fax 843-853-0044
E-mail sales@arcadiapublishing.com
For customer service and orders:
Toll-Free 1-888-313-2665

Visit us on the Internet at www.arcadiapublishing.com

Dedicated to Deb,
who has climbed the mountain with me
through fire and rain.

CONTENTS

ACKNOWLEDGMENTS

I would like to thank all of the people who helped me in the preparation of this book: Debra McGeehan for her tireless work at every stage of the process, without whom this book would not have been possible; Georgeanne Freeburg for her contacts, editing, and historical knowledge; Glenn Freeburg for his historical knowledge of Johnsonburg and its past and for the use of his photographs; Mark Wendel for the use of his photographs; Marie Biel, local historian; Ron King and Domtar Inc. for their knowledge of the paper mill and its past; John Imbrogno, Carl Imbrogno, and Louis Imbrogno for their lifetime of memories of working at the mill and growing up in Johnsonburg; Bill and Mike Bauer for their knowledge of railroads and photographs; Dave Woods; Tim Leathers; Steve Michuck; Yvonne McKinney Michuck; Thomas Folino; John Fedorko; Krista Zameroski; Mary Kalinowski, director of the Elk County Historical Society, for the use of photographs; Dr. Vernon Ordiway and the staff of the Elk County Historical Society for their valuable archival work; John T. and Elizabeth D. McGeehan; Edgar and Dorothy Schnarrs; Rebecca Clayton; and Erin Vosgien, my publisher, for her patience and guidance.

All photographs, unless otherwise noted, are courtesy of the Elk County Historical Society.

INTRODUCTION

Johnsonburg is the heart of Elk County. The very word Johnsonburg has always meant something to area residents. It is the mill. The mill is the dynamic heart of Elk County that keeps on pumping. It gathers essential fluids from the arteries of Elk County, the East and West Branches of the Clarion River. Raw materials of wood, to be made into paper, funnel into the mill to leave as paper to carry the words and pictures to inform the nation. As the nation's tastes have changed, the mill has pumped stronger or weaker. The mill has been slow and has hummed with powerful regularity. As the industrial workplace became more automated, Johnsonburg's economy declined. The residents have become the heart and strength of the county. Johnsonburg residents have always had a fierce loyalty to their community. The aroma of sulfur that sometimes suffuses the air in Johnsonburg has different connotations to local residents. It means prosperity, employment, continuation, and survival. In the past, the river suffered from industrial runoff. The Clarion River today is a shining example of progress. The waters of the Clarion once again flow pure due to careful upgrading of environmental standards over the years. The ripples of the pristine river today once again evoke the primitive, emotional clarion call of the river. In the 1980s, the mill was totally modernized to become the largest, continuous-process building in the world. It is an awesome sight, this industrial giant. The main highway route through Johnsonburg goes right through the center of the mill. You cannot go through "'Burg" without driving through the heart of this industrial giant.

Johnsonburg is located at the confluence of the two major branches of the Clarion River. The juncture of the East and the West Branches of the Clarion River was the natural place that the earliest explorers utilized. In 1810, a settler named David Johnson was known to inhabit the forks of the upper Clarion. Johnson was a hunter, trapper, and fisherman who maintained a sod house and garden in the vicinity of the place that would later bear his name. Not much is known about the mysterious Johnson. It is assumed that he was associated with Benjamin Cooper, land speculator from New Jersey. In 1784, the Iroquois chief Cornplanter sold this area of land to the State of Pennsylvania, which opened it up for bids. The Holland Land Company resold a tract of land to Benjamin Cooper. Cooper visited the land, and Johnson may have been affiliated with him. The enterprise was originally to be named Cooperstown. In 1821, when Jacob Ridgway opened up a settlement 10 miles downstream, Johnson abandoned what he considered the overpopulated hunting grounds to move his family further west.

The availability of wood, waterpower, sandstone, and natural gas made the location prosper. The river was known variously as Coopers Creek, Big Toby Creek, Stump Creek, and finally the Clarion River. It was ideal for industrial development, but the impression of the place for many years was one of impenetrable wilderness filled with wild animals and poisonous snakes. After 50 years of inactivity, Lyman Wilmarth built a water-powered sawmill in 1852 on the West Branch to move lumber to Pittsburgh, and the area became known as Wilmarth. The road from Johnsonburg to Wilcox intersects the Milesburg–Smethport Turnpike at Tambine. However, better transportation was needed to move Johnsonburg's timber products to markets. In the 1850s, Thomas L. Kane, the developer and founder of the famed Civil War Bucktail regiment, was instrumental in bringing the Sunbury and Erie Railroad through Johnsonburg. This railroad eventually became the Philadelphia and Erie and later the Pennsylvania Railroad. In 1880, the Pittsburgh and New York Railroad, later named Buffalo, Rochester and Pittsburgh, and eventually Baltimore and Ohio Railroad (B&O), came through Johnsonburg. When the New York, Lake Erie and Western Railroad, later the Erie Railroad, also entered Johnsonburg, the town became an important rail center. Logs and lumber that formerly were rafted or driven down the river could now have rail access to many new markets. The new rail connections also brought in many new Italian, Swedish, and Polish immigrants.

The area became known as Quay, after Pennsylvania's senator and political boss, when they needed a name for a post office. The name lasted only one year, and in 1889, the borough of Johnsonburg was incorporated and named after the first settler. Johnsonburg's destiny was created in 1888 when Mylert M. Armstrong Sr. started the Clarion Pulp and Paper Company. In 1889, the new mill was almost destroyed by flooding, but the infant industry would survive to become the largest paper mill in the country, still in business after 120 years. The mill was renamed the New York and Pennsylvania Company in 1890. The giant mill was an impressive sight, as the pulpwood was stacked in 30-foot-high piles for one mile up the Silver Creek valley and huge piles of sawdust up the East Branch valley. The forests funneled in timber by rail to be queued up in pulpwood stacks. Small locomotives called dinkeys shuttled pulp to the chippers, and sawdust was spit out the other end of the mill with rolls of paper continuing their journey by rail. The mill underwent another name change to the Castanea Company when the Curtis Publishing empire of Philadelphia bought controlling interest in the mill in 1925. The mill became the largest manufacturer of magazine paper in the world to furnish Curtis's flagship publications: the *Saturday Evening Post* and the *Ladies' Home Journal*. The U.S. government was the mill's second-biggest customer. As the mill's machinery was modernized and made safer, the workplace saw fewer and fewer of the one-armed papermakers, which had been the badge of the profession. The Armstrong Forest Company was eventually created to invest in timberlands to supply the mill, eventually purchasing forestlands in Canada. When magazine publishing declined in this country, the Curtis Publishing Company went out of business and the mill became PennTech, Weyerhauser, Willamette, and now Domtar. Nearby Wilcox was once the site of the world's largest tannery.

In 1921, the New York and Pennsylvania Company built the Johnsonburg Community Building, which became the social center for Johnsonburg's citizens. It also built Johnsonburg Memorial Field, where the competitive athletes of Johnsonburg have won many contests over the years.

Today Johnsonburg is within the new Pennsylvania Wilds tourism area. One of the recreational jewels of this wild and scenic region is the East Branch Dam, built in the early 1950s to remedy the devastating flooding that the area was prone to. The six-mile-long lake, surrounded by state forestlands and state game lands, reflects the wilderness character that is the region's heritage.

The high point of Johnsonburg's prosperity was World War I. After the war, newer technologies outmoded many of Johnsonburg's older industries, and devastating floods in 1936 and 1942 hit the community hard. Through these troubling times, the mill survived and was the backbone of the area economy invigorating Johnsonburg's life. Many names have flowed through Johnsonburg's history. One must believe that the early mountain man the town is named after would be proud of his namesake community that survives as the heart of Elk County.

One

EARLY INDUSTRIES

The Johnsonburg paper mill had a huge appetite for pulpwood and devoured entire forests. Before 1925, the wood was obtained locally from the Elk County area. After that date, the mill bought property and brought wood in from the southern states, New York, the Upper Peninsula of Michigan, and Canada.

Tall, strong, rugged trees could only be tamed by tall, strong, rugged men. Men that matched the strength of the land and the unbroken forest were the first settlers that cleared the upper branches of the Clarion River and carved out a life for themselves and their families in this wilderness.

A barkpeeler has used a spud to remove the valuable bark from a tree to make it easier for the axmen to fell this forest giant. Hard hats or safety glasses were undreamed of luxuries far in the future for these early lumberjacks. Loggers, often immigrants, were young and willing to work long hours. There was plenty of work available.

These lumberjacks show off the tools of their trade: a crosscut saw, double-bitted axe, spud, maul, wedge, and peavey for rolling logs. The photographer has captured these wood hicks taking a smoke break amid some very sizable timber. A few simple tools and lots of human muscle power converted vast forests into fortunes for some, usually not the wielders of the muscle power.

At the end of a hard day in the woods, timbermen were only too happy to oblige the photographer by posing around and on top of a large rock showing off their trusty crosscut saws. Note the ramshackle camp in the right background and its shaky-rigged heating apparatus.

A lumbering crew is shown taking a break for a group portrait amid the jumble and clutter that was the wood hick's life in the forest. Logs were hauled to a rail siding for transport. This rail line looks like it is under construction in the foreground. Note the man shouldering the crosscut saw and the little girl with ribbons in her hair in background at the far left.

Lumberjacks, or wood hicks, were a hardy lot that endured the hard work of clearing the big forests. However, after a challenging day's work, they sometimes relaxed for a smoke or to listen to one of their own entertain on the squeeze-box amid the chaos that they had created in the forest behind them using great logs as benches. Music has charms to captivate concert halls and forest clearings.

12

These loggers with their team of horses are dwarfed by the clear-cut hillside behind them. They seem undaunted by the herculean task at hand. Profit and not environmental issues was the motivation of these businessmen. When one looks at the forests of Elk County today, one is amazed at how quickly and efficiently nature recovers.

Here is an example of one of the many splash dams that were built throughout Elk County by the timbering industry to facilitate the moving of logs. When all of the small dams were released, or dynamited in some cases, the resulting flood moved logs downstream to be made into timber rafts, to railroad sidings, or to be cut in sawmills. (Mark Wendel.)

This is a photograph of a log slide. Lumberjacks sometimes built these devices to facilitate the moving of cut timber through rough, uneven terrain. It was faster than dragging the logs with horses where there was enough volume to be practical. The idea was to build a chute to slide the logs along. This example has a path alongside for the loggers to guide the logs down the slide.

Here is another example of a log slide. This one is rather steep and the slide even has higher rails to keep the logs from flying off the chute. Flying logs became dangerous projectiles that could injure and did occasionally kill lumberjacks. They also damaged valuable standing timber. Examples have been noted where a flying log smashed completely through the trunk of a standing tree.

This pair of horses is capable of moving this heavy load due to the deep snow and the slippery conditions. Without snow, a horse could drag only one log at a time. Note that in this photograph, there is another team of horses following this one and a large pile of logs waiting to be moved. Note the gentleman in the long beard and topcoat, possibly an overseer.

Seven teams of horses are employed at this large log yard. Note the crosswise smaller logs on the log pile arranged so logs can be rolled easier to be loaded. All of the men are leaning on peaveys, a tool designed specifically to roll logs. Logs were very heavy, and extreme vigilance was necessary to avoid injuries to man and beast. (Dave Woods.)

Here is a scene of hemlock bark being loaded onto railroad cars from horse-drawn carts. The wood hicks eye the photographer suspiciously. Note that a huge log stripped of its bark is used to fill the gap between the rail car and horse wagon while another log is ready. The men are using a big stump as a workbench to store their jug and tools.

Timber tract owners usually managed the nonwoods end of the business, but sometimes they ventured out into the forest to oversee the timber cutting. None may have looked as out of place as this sport wearing fancy pants, a suit and tie, and snap-brim hat and smoking a pipe. A corduroy road and a log slide are also in evidence.

Here is a scene of the building of a logging spur using stringer track. Rails would be laid on top of these logs. There were many of these narrow-gauge logging spurs throughout the state to get logs out of steep drainages. Railroad building was an essential part of the lumbering business.

Horses were more common on the job at lumbering sites, but oxen were also used. In this scene, workers are building one of the many narrow-gauge railroads that twisted up most of the narrow valleys of north-central Pennsylvania to get the timber out. Traces of these old rail lines can still be found in many of the valleys of the area.

Log loaders were used to load logs from a siding after horses had dragged the logs out of the woods. The loader is seen here loading a railcar. A man is seen guiding the log with a bar. These men had to be nimble and ever vigilant to avoid being crushed by the heavy logs. Many accidents happened in this business.

A log loader is shown in action in this image. In the narrow valleys of mountainous north-central Pennsylvania, it was impossible to build a double-track width. The loader is on the rails with cars to its front and rear. This machine loads cars to its front and then swings around and lifts another car from its rear to be moved and loaded. This scene shows one of the cars in midair.

18

A Glen Hazel and Shawmut Railroad log train is seen pulling a load of logs near Glen Hazel. There is a large crew of men riding the train on the logs. When log loaders came into use, only three men were needed to load logs. This scene is obviously before that innovation. The East Branch of the Clarion River is on the left.

This is the millpond for the Dolliver sawmill at Glen Hazel. In the right foreground, Crooked Creek has been dammed up to form the pond. In the left background is the railroad, which delivered logs to the mill. A well-constructed ramp for unloading logs is at the left, although logs are obviously also rolled down the slope beyond. The mill burned in 1895, as was the fate of many of these wooden structures.

Hemlock bark for the area tanneries became so valuable that at the end of the logging boom, only the bark was harvested. The logs were left lying in the woods. In this scene, woodsmen are using horse carts and a corduroy road to deliver bark to be loaded onto a railroad car. A corduroy road keeps the horse teams out of the mud.

Here is a wintertime scene of crews with teams of horses loading pulpwood onto railcars. The Johnsonburg paper mill was voracious in its need for pulpwood and eventually, after cutting the entire area around the mill in 1925, pulpwood had to be brought in from New York State, Canada, and the southern states. Note the clear-cut landscape in the background of this photograph.

Here is a logging locomotive hauling several flatcars loaded with wood over a small creek spanned by a trestle. A small group of onlookers is wondering what the photographer's interest is in this typical scene. The woods of north-central Pennsylvania had many uses. Wood was used for construction, tanning, railroad ties, mine props, chemicals, pulp for paper, furniture, plus many other assorted uses.

Lumbering was the first big industry of the county, and timber made many fortunes. Lumber camps were self-contained little communities of laborers working in the deep forest. Many of the camps employed a single ethnic immigrant group so that they would work well together. The workers often took trains into nearby towns on weekends for church and social life, one as solemn as the other was wild.

Horses were the heavy lifters of the timber industry. They dragged logs out of the woods, pulled bark wagons to the rail sidings, and even acted as transportation through the woods. A good horse wrangler was a very valuable employee to the timbering industry, and each took great pride in the look and quality of their charges, posing here for a photograph.

The entire lumber camp has turned out to get into the photograph. There are men on the roof, in the doorways, and poking out of an upstairs window. This camp is located at a railroad juncture as tracks arrive from two directions. The juncture is center, left. The clearing is a clutter of crude structures, barrels, bark, logs, wood chips, sawdust, slashings, and wood hicks.

Another typical sawmill view shows the crew posing for the cameraman. Many of these camps and mills were photographed to record the mill because they knew that the operations were seasonal and temporary, moving on after an area had been cut. This mill is surrounded by wood debris. Note the elevated track to bring in materials and the man poking out of the upstairs window.

Lumberjacks, or wood hicks, lived in unpainted crude buildings because the camps' utility lasted only until the area was cut. This camp even has some unframed windows. The camps usually had female cooks. The young boy sitting on the man's knee on the right has picked some wildflowers to brighten up the drab quarters.

A girl watches another emptying a dustpan out of an upstairs window. A woman with a washbasin watches an older woman scold a young girl emptying a pail. Too posed to be real, it still illustrates the typical lumber camp well. They were simple and utilitarian. Notice that they did not even cut the planks on the roof to make them even. Credit the photographer for the interesting domestic scene.

Here is a sawmill in the Burning Well area. The millpond is filled with logs waiting to be cut. The locomotive has delivered the logs. Note the wooden skids that have been constructed to allow the logs to be rolled off the side of the railcars and into the millpond. Everyone in the scene, including the people on the porch of the residential home, is aware of the photographer.

Here is a view of Rolfe, which was absorbed into Johnsonburg in 1952. Most of the view is taken up by the Henry, Bayard and Company's sawmill and lumberyard. The Methodist church, which stood until 1969, is at the left and beside it is the Rolfe School, which stood half in Johnsonburg and half in Rolfe and eventually burned. West Center Street runs through the center of the photograph.

Here is the interior of a typical planing mill. Rough lumber was finished into useful sizes for the building trades. Stacked lumber, belted machines, various tools hanging from the walls, and a storage loft all illustrate the business. Sawdust littered the building, and fire was a constant hazard. Lumber was needed for local construction as well as for export out of the area.

Emil Carlson is shown using a bark spud to remove bark from a hemlock log in the Tambine area. Hemlock bark is high in tannic acid and was used in tanneries to process hides into leather. Wagonloads of bark were a common scene in the region. There were tanneries throughout Elk County, Wilcox once having the world's largest tannery. Many buffalo hides from the west were processed in local tanneries.

The Tannery near Rolfe.
Johnsonburg, Pa.

Before becoming part of Johnsonburg borough, Rolfe was a separate community. Industrial growth in the Johnsonburg area started when Stephen Kistler and sons started a tannery at Rolfe. The tannery employed 100 men and produced 1,500 hides per week while using 12,000 cords of hemlock bark weekly. Some 57 company houses were built and supplied with light and heat from gas wells drilled on company property. (Mark Wendel.)

Here is the Rolfe Tannery, left center. The Baltimore and Ohio Railroad (B&O) tracks and trestle can be seen coming down the East Branch valley with the Pennsylvania Railroad tracks and trestle passing underneath it. The large building at the right is the bleach plant of the paper mill with the "Tannery Row" houses in front of it. The juncture of the rivers is just out of the photograph to the right.

A tannery beam house was where flesh was removed from animal hides. It was a place of noxious odors and foul liquid seepage and took a strong stomach. The place of work was a labyrinth of overhead ropes, wires, pulleys, and reeking hides. A solution of water and chicken manure was used to remove the hair from the hides. These men seem to be acclimated to the odoriferous climate.

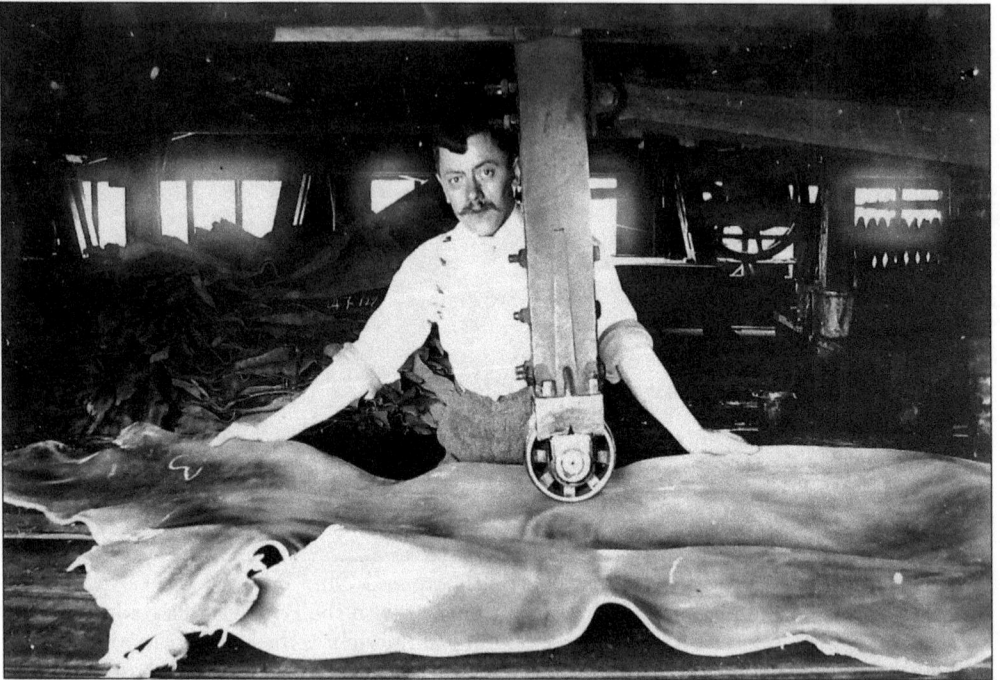

Wherever there was logging, there were tanneries, which used one of the by-products of the timber industry, hemlock bark. In this photograph, a worker at the Instanter Tannery is working the animal hide into leather after the hair had been removed and it had been steeped in a vat of tannic acid.

Workers at Instanter take a break to pose for a photograph. These workers appear to be wheelwrights. Instanter was an isolated community deep in the forest, but it was served by the Johnsonburg and Clermont Railroad (a branch of the Pennsylvania Railroad). It also had narrow-gauge railroads to deliver logs to its sawmill and bark to its tannery so there was plenty of work for wheelwrights.

Coopers were men who built barrels. In the past, barrels were used in almost every field and good coopers were valuable workers. A well-made barrel was a work of functional art that was usually unnoticed. These coopers take a break from their work schedule to pose, sitting on their work with some of their tools and product in the background.

This miner has carried authenticity to the extreme for his studio portrait. He is posing in a crawling position with his pick to duplicate conditions in the mine where shafts were dug no larger than they needed to be. He also has his carbide headlamp lit. However he is not even on the photographer's backdrop, which is wildly inappropriate for the interior of a mine.

This is a view of the Yingling-Martin Brick Company, including its clay pits, right, in Johnsonburg. It was located on the south end of town along the Ridgway Road, Route 219. The houses at the upper left are located on Powers Avenue along Powers Run on the St. Marys Road, Route 255. After an extended period of operation, this plant was forced to close due to competition from newer building materials. (Mark Wendel.)

This is a view of the brick works at Deckertown at the south end of Johnsonburg. Many of the bricks used to build Johnsonburg were produced locally. There was an early sun-dried brick plant at the location of the community building. When stone, concrete, glass, and steel replaced bricks, this business ended. Deckertown was named after John Piper Decker, who developed East Street and Powers Avenue. (Mark Wendel.)

The subject of this photograph is the early brickyard known as the Terra Cotta Brick Works in Johnsonburg. The plant made vitrified brick for paving. Elk County was blessed with much clay, and clay-product factories were scattered around the county. Cement and crushed stone replaced paving bricks for road building, and the industry is gone today.

A standard-gauge Climax locomotive of a logging operation is pictured. The occupation of the men can be assumed from their dress. An engineer in overalls, a fireman in white shirt and cap, a station agent in white shirt and three loggers in suspenders hitching a ride to the woods are all lounging on the train for a photograph.

Sam Irwin is at the throttle of a locomotive on the Erie Railroad at the Clarion Junction in Johnsonburg. The coal tipple can be seen in the left background. Johnsonburg was an important rail center and used by three different lines: the Pennsylvania Railroad, the B&O and the Erie Railroad plus mill switching tracks. It was estimated that there were 17 miles of railroads inside Johnsonburg borough. (Bill Bauer.)

This is the scene at the Clarion Junction during the flood of 1942. Note the high water in the East Branch of the Clarion River and the submerged vehicle at the lower right. Rail traffic was not interrupted for long as the work crews were fast and efficient. The Erie Railroad is in the foreground, and the B&O is in the background. (Steve Michuck.)

The Pennsylvania Railroad station is shown in front of the Armstrong Hotel in Johnsonburg. Evidently a passenger train has just pulled away as disembarked travelers have boarded an early automobile for delivery to their hotel. Freight and wagons are also in evidence as bystanders await the next arrival. The smokestacks of the paper mill are in the left background. Johnsonburg was a busy hub of railroading in times past. (Mark Wendel.)

Trains have infinite capacity to fascinate small boys and old boys. Train wrecks are even more of an attraction. This derailed train lying on its side has drawn out two youths, dressed in the fashion of their day, to rubberneck at the mishap. Train wrecks were a constant fear in the days when that mode of travel and hauling were the most common method.

Besides damaging many Johnsonburg homes and the paper mill, the severe flood of 1942 played havoc with the Pennsylvania Railroad. Rolling stock and roadbeds were extensively damaged. Here a Pennsylvania Railroad inspector surveys the damage to begin repair work. In the left background, it is evident that the floodwaters have not receded yet.

This wide-angle view shows Johnsonburg, right, and the paper mill, left. The Clarion River is flowing in front of both. The Pennsylvania Railroad trestle at the river juncture is at left. Between the river and the mill is the Flats section of town. At the lower right, on the near side of the river is the Black Works, which made carbon for paint pigments and other purposes. That business eventually burned.

Two

THE PAPER MILL

1926

In 1926, the Johnsonburg mill was known as the Castanea Company. Here it is shown spewing volumes of smoke from the numerous stacks of the industrial giant. The Clarion River, seen in the foreground, used to receive much industrial runoff from the mill. Today the mill has been upgraded to modern environmental standards and the air and water quality in the area are much improved.

An overall view of the Johnsonburg paper mill in the early 20th century shows the mill, center, and the town, right. The Pennsylvania and B&O railroad bridges can be seen crossing the juncture of the Clarion River branches at the left. The Grant Avenue Ballfield in the Flats section is in use at the lower right. (Mark Wendel.)

This is the East Branch of the Clarion River running through the mill. Note the large pile of pulpwood ready to be fed to the chipper via the elevated conveyor. The square building at the foot of the bridge on the left side was moved back to make way for the main office of the mill. (Mark Wendel.)

Here is the old metal bridge that used to carry Center Street, the main street running through town, over the East Branch of the Clarion River. This bridge was replaced by a concrete span but traffic still moved through the very center of the mill. Today a bypass is being built to carry Route 219 around the mill. The main office of the mill is seen at the lower left. (Mark Wendel.)

This view of Johnsonburg shows the paper mill, center, and the Flats section of town, bottom. The Flats was destroyed by the flood of 1942 and never rebuilt. The tall building in the center is the Sulphite Mill. The Pennsylvania Railroad and its boxcars can be seen in front of the mill. (Mark Wendel.)

Here is a view of the south end of the Johnsonburg paper mill. The tall building on the right is the Sulphite Mill. The Pennsylvania Railroad tracks can be seen on the left side of the building and in the distance on the left is the B&O trestle over the West Branch of the Clarion River. The tracks on the right are mill-switching tracks. (Mark Wendel.)

Smokestacks dominate this view of the New York and Pennsylvania Company paper mill in Johnsonburg. The main office building is at left where the white bridge carries Center Street over the East Branch of the Clarion River. The black bridge below that is the Pennsylvania Railroad's bridge at the juncture of the East and West Branches. The large building with the lettering behind the boxcars is the machine shop.

This view is of the Clarion Mill, center, and Highland Mill, left background, units of the New York and Pennsylvania Paper Company in Johnsonburg. The Pennsylvania Railroad separates the mill from the Flats area in the foreground. The Pennsylvania Railroad trestle, left foreground, is located at the juncture of the East and West Branches of the Clarion River. Market Street and the downtown are visible on the right.

This scene shows how the Johnsonburg mill and town functioned side by side. The Flats section of town can be seen growing right up to the mill along the Clarion River on the right. The B&O tracks can be seen in the foreground, and the Pennsylvania Railroad is right up against the mill.

The B&O trestle is seen crossing the West Branch of the Clarion. The buildings in the center are along the East Branch, and the main stem of the river starts at their juncture on the right. In the left center, a short white bridge can be seen that carries Center Street across the east branch at the main office of the mill. (Mark Wendel.)

Birds Eye View of Johnsonburg, Pa.
looking towards the B. R. & P. R. R. Siding.

This view of Johnsonburg is looking up the West Branch of the Clarion River. The B&O trestle can be traced bisecting the paper mill. The tall building in the center is the Sulphite Mill. The Hotel Johnsonburg and the Armstrong Hotel can be seen on the left. The downtown area is bottom center, and the Avenues is at the lower right. (Mark Wendel.)

The Buffalo, Rochester and Pittsburgh, later the B&O, trestle is seen crossing the West Branch of the Clarion River and the Johnsonburg mill complex. The Highland Pulp Mill, center, and the Clarion Paper Mill, right, both became part of the New York and Pennsylvania Company. The Pennsylvania Railroad tracks and Center Street cross under the trestle, and the Erie Railroad tracks are in the distance. (Mark Wendel.)

This is the Highland Mill section of the paper mill located along what is today Glen Avenue where it is joined by First Avenue. The Vennard Island Bridge is on the left of the photograph, and below that is the Erie Railroad bridge over the East Branch. The Johnsonburg Railroad goes up the valley on the far side of the river, and boxcars can be seen on the right. (Mark Wendel.)

This industrial complex is the Johnsonburg paper mill, located at the juncture of the East and West Branches of the Clarion River and spanned by the Pennsylvania Railroad trestle at lower left. At the upper left is a B&O locomotive chugging up the East Branch valley. The Center Street Bridge crosses the East Branch at the main office of the mill. The town of Johnsonburg is in the upper right.

The Pennsylvania Railroad trestle at the juncture of the rivers can be seen at the left. The buildings along the Clarion River are the machine shop (on the left) and the paper machine rooms (on the right). Behind them in the center, the tall building is the Soda Recovery Building. The Avenues area of Johnsonburg is in the right background.

This Johnsonburg paper mill view shows the Soda Recovery Building, the tall building at left, and the Sulphite Mill, the tall building on the right. Between them is the machine shop building. The Pennsylvania Railroad trestle crosses the rivers at the juncture, center, and above that is the Center Street Bridge and an elevated tramway over the East Branch. The B&O tracks can be seen at lower left.

The B&O trestle is shown crossing the West Branch of the Clarion River and going through the Johnsonburg paper mill. The tall building, center, is the Soda Recovery Building, located on the bank of the East Branch, built in 1951 and imploded in 1994. In the right background is the Avenues section of Johnsonburg. (Mark Wendel.)

The paper mill dominates this view of Johnsonburg. The residential section and First Avenue can be seen at the bottom of the photograph. The large building at left is Sulphite Mill and the tall building at right is the Soda Recovery Building. The large black triangle at right is coal used to fuel the mill through the main power building seen just above it with five smokestacks.

Here is an overall view of Johnsonburg, dominated by the paper mill. The two branches of the Clarion River enter from the right and merge at the mill. Along the West Branch at top right is Johnsonburg's west end and the separate community of Rolfe at the far right. Rolfe has since been incorporated into Johnsonburg borough.

This handsome redbrick building has been the main office of the Johnsonburg paper mill through many name changes. It is located on Center Street at the East Branch of the Clarion River. It has often been flooded. Railroad tracks on both sides of the building were used to shuttle wood to the mill. (Mark Wendel.)

This is a very early view of Johnsonburg. The Pennsylvania Railroad trestle crosses the Clarion River where the two branches join. The old metal Center Street Bridge can be seen on the East Branch, left. On the right, the original wood frame Holy Rosary Church on Market Street and the wooden school on First Avenue can be seen.

Here the East Branch comes in from the bottom, and the West Branch from the right to form the Clarion River flowing to the top left. The white bridge is Center Street, above that is an elevated conveyor and above that is the Pennsylvania Railroad trestle. To their right is the B&O trestle crossing the West Branch. Grant Street crosses the Clarion at the baseball diamond, upper left.

This view of the Johnsonburg paper mill is along the East Branch of the Clarion River. The tall building at left is the Soda Recovery Building, and the building with five black smokestacks is the old power plant. Below that is Sulphite Mill. The intersection of Center and Cobb Streets in downtown Johnsonburg can be seen at the right.

In 1968, PennTech Papers took over the Johnsonburg paper mill. Today Domtar owns the mill, and its letters have replaced the ones on this building at the corner of Center and Cobb Streets. The building on the left is now gone as well as the large dust collector attached to the building. Today this building is the main powerhouse of the paper mill.

This is a view of Johnsonburg from the heights on Water Street. The tall building, center, is the Soda Recovery Building of the paper mill. There are numerous piles of wood where the Knothole baseball fields are located today. The square building with the peaked roof, center right, is the Rolfe Methodist Church. The large building in the center left is the mill warehouse. (Mark Wendel.)

The pulpwood yard stretched for a mile up the Silver Creek valley. A narrow-gauge railroad was built for access to the towering piles of pulpwood. The railroad was dismantled and moved as needed to get to a new pile. The yard was abandoned in 1971 when the Sulphite Mill was closed, and pulp was no longer shipped in by rail and stored.

Here is a scene of the pulpwood yard at the Johnsonburg paper mill. Large conveyors form the pulpwood into stacks ready to be transferred into the mill by the railroad snaking through the colossal mounds where they will go through the chipper to be made into paper. The large piles of pulpwood and steaming piles of sawdust were always a colorful sight along the Silver Creek valley in Rolfe.

These are wood pulp stackers for the Johnsonburg paper mill. Railroads were constructed to deliver pulpwood to the Silver Creek valley in Rolfe for the mill. When one pile was high enough, the railroad was moved to an empty section and a new pile was started. The mill operated continuously, and a dinkey engine delivered pulp to the chipper to be ground up for paper.

New paper mill employees almost always started in the pulpwood yard and worked in both summer heat and freezing winter storms. Note the person sitting on top of this woodpile. It was not the safest perch. There were also enormous sawdust piles generated by the mill. It was not the safest playground for area youths.

These are papermaking machines and their operators at the Johnsonburg paper mill. It was a hot, dusty, noisy environment in which to work, surrounded by numerous machines with moving parts and safety standards far in the future. Note the very young age of some of the employees. One gentleman in the center of this photograph is wearing a suit. (Mark Wendel.)

This scene shows soda pulp machines in the Highland Pulp and Paper Company in Johnsonburg. The workers appear to be quite young in this photograph. Wood fiber was beaten into liquid and then rolled into various types of paper by rows and rows of machines. Safety standards have improved considerably since this primitive era.

These are papermaking machines and their operators at the Johnsonburg paper mill. The Curtis Publishing Company of Philadelphia owned the mill for a time and produced its paper here. Curtis published high-quality magazines and periodicals. At one time, the Johnsonburg paper mill produced the most glossy magazine paper of any mill in the world.

These men are beating wood pulp into a liquid form to be made into paper at the Johnsonburg paper mill. This labor-intensive work was eventually automated by hydro-pulpers, but it was not until 1940 that this job became obsolete. The beater room was a maze of overhead pipes and tubing.

Johnsonburg is known as the "Paper City," and at one time, it was the largest producer of magazine paper in the world. It supplied Curtis Publishing Company's flagship periodicals, the *Saturday Evening Post* and the *Ladies' Home Journal*. Although magazine publishing has declined, and the mill has changed hands and names many times, it endures. The mill has been modernized to meet the times and flourishes at the heart of Johnsonburg.

This is the teamsters building or horse barn of the Johnsonburg mill. Although the mill had miles of railroad switching tracks inside the complex, the mill was so vast that there was plenty of hauling work for teams of horses. There were also jobs for that special breed of man from the past that had a special affinity for handling working horses or mules.

The dinkey engine was used in the paper mill yard to move wood from the wood yard through a tunnel to the mill. The two outside black domes on the top are sand domes used to funnel sand onto the wheels when greater traction is needed. One of the operators is holding an oilcan, a necessity to keep these iron behemoths running. They still squealed a lot.

Here are the flood-swollen branches of the Clarion River during the flood of 1942: West Branch, bottom, and East Branch, center. The Center Street Bridge has collapsed in front of the main office building. Across the East Branch is the bleach plant and in front of that, some of the old Tannery Row houses are still standing. The old power plant's five smokestacks are seen in the right background.

Looking up the East Branch of the Clarion River during the flood of 1942 this image shows the high water that has taken out the Center Street Bridge. The building on the left bank is the old bleach plant, which has been removed, and across the river from that, the corner of the paper mill's main office is visible.

This view is looking north at the south end of the paper mill during the flood of 1942. The Flats area is on the left and the paper machine building is in the center background. A large tank has been floated randomly as well as piles of wood debris. The railroad tracks have been buckled and twisted. Transportation in the area was disrupted for some time.

This scene is in the Vennard Island section of the Johnsonburg paper mill from the flood of 1942 and shows damage to the Erie Railroad. Several boxcars have been floated off of the tracks. However, the bridge was not destroyed as the Pennsylvania Railroad trestle was downstream. This view is looking up the East Branch valley.

The flood of 1942 took out the Center Street Bridge, which carries Route 219 over the East Branch of the Clarion River and is the main artery north and south for the Johnsonburg area. It also connects the two parts of Johnsonburg borough. It was a major disruption to life in this riverside community. The main office of the paper mill is on the left edge of the photograph.

Johnsonburg and its mill complex have often been flooded because of its location beside two rivers. Over the years, the mill workers have developed strategies for coping with high water. In this photograph, the workers have built temporary wooden sluices to carry water out of the mill and back into its channel. During several years, all of the best strategies of men could not hold back nature.

In this photograph a Johnsonburg mill worker is holding both hands on top of his head in disbelief at the damage caused by the great flood of 1942. The water was gone, but the mud was everywhere. The mill complex was a maze of lanes, rails, tanks, smokestacks, overhead conveyors, and pipes. The pipes in this photograph are steam lines from the main power plant.

56

Here is a scene from the flood of 1942 looking south on Center Street. The Center Street Bridge over the East Branch has been taken out by floodwaters, and spectators wade through mud to view the spectacle. The main office building is center left and across the river is the bleach plant. In front of that building is the black dinkey engine used to haul wood to the mill.

Two mill workers stand by a tank along Center Street that has been floated off its site by the flood of 1942. The Sulphite Mill is in the background. There were rumors that a chlorine tank had sprung a dangerous leak and the area would be evacuated, but fortunately safety teams secured all of the mills' hazardous materials.

This scene is from the flood of 1942. Massive cleanup was needed after the water receded. There was a shortage of heavy equipment, and much of the debris removal had to be done by hand. The high water floated all kinds of refuse and left it behind in every nook and cranny of the mill. No employees were laid off. They were just redirected to the cleanup effort.

Duck Rock is on the hillside of Clarion Heights. The stone for the foundation of the paper mill was quarried in this area, as was the stone for the Pennsylvania Railroad's beautiful multiarch bridge at Rockville near Harrisburg. There are also ancient Native American carvings on rocks in the area. Today a highway bypass will finally reroute traffic over this hillside, and traffic will no longer go through the mill. Johnsonburg is visible at the lower right.

Three

JOHNSONBURG

In this aerial view, the West Branch comes in from the left, and the East Branch flows in from the upper right to form the Clarion River, bottom. The Johnsonburg paper mill is at the juncture of the rivers, and the town is on the right. In 1942, a devastating flood destroyed all of the housing from the Flats below the Pennsylvania Railroad tracks at the bottom of this scene.

This is an aerial view of downtown Johnsonburg. The Brick Block along Market Street is prominent in the middle of the scene. The Glen Hazel Road is seen curving out of the photograph at the top. Other notable buildings are the Johnsonburg School (center, right), Ubel and Flynn Furniture and Undertaking (white building, bottom center), the Johnsonburg Community Building (bottom, right), and the Holy Rosary Church (bottom, right).

In this early view of Johnsonburg, the Brick Block along Market Street and the Armstrong Hotel are prominent. Holy Rosary Church's first wood frame building on Market Street is visible on the left, and a large wooden derrick is on Center Street. Bridge Street goes up the hill and is intersected by First Avenue. The isolated building halfway up the empty First Avenue was mill official John A. Craig's mansion.

Here is a bird's-eye view of Johnsonburg looking southeast. The Clarion River is in the foreground, and the Powers Run Valley is at the top right. The Armstrong Opera House and the Armstrong Hotel are prominent on the left, and the Grant Street Bridge is visible on the right. In front of the Armstrong Hotel is the Pennsylvania Railroad station, and in front of that is the section of town known as the Flats.

In this view of Johnsonburg looking east, the Clarion River is in the foreground with its bridge crossing it. The Armstrong Hotel is prominent at the left center with the buildings on Market Street behind it. Between the river and the downtown area, the Pennsylvania Railroad crosses the middle of the photograph with its station at the far left. (Mark Wendel.)

Here is Johnsonburg with the mill on the left and the downtown on the right. The Armstrong Hotel towers above the cityscape. The Clarion River Bridge is in the left foreground. At the bottom right, laundry can be seen hanging on the line outside a residence. The Railroad Crossing sign warns, "Look out for the cars," although whether it is warning trains or automobiles is unclear. (Glenn Freeburg.)

The International Order of Odd Fellows was a vigorous fraternal club in times past and often held parades in many towns. Here they have garlanded Market Street in Johnsonburg with arches at each end of the street for some festive occasion. The Hyatt Pharmaceutical Building is on the left and the Johnsonburg National Bank, draped in bunting is on the right. The street is still unpaved with wooden sidewalks. (Mark Wendel.)

Market Street, Johnsonburg, Pa.

A lone pedestrian stands on the corner of Market Street and Bridge Street looking out for nonexistent traffic at a totally empty downtown intersection. Several men can be seen conversing on the corner of the Brick Block. Although not troubled by traffic yet, the downtown in this scene has recently added streetlights and brick street paving. (Mark Wendel.)

Two investors are pictured coming out of the Johnsonburg National Bank. The bank was chartered in 1891 by a group that included Mylert M. Armstrong Sr. They built a two-story grey stone building at the corner of Market and Bridge Streets at a cost of $20,000. The building has been a fixture at the downtown intersection ever since, and while undergoing many corporate name changes, has always been used as a bank. (Mark Wendel.)

63

The north side of Market Street in Johnsonburg was known as the Brick Block. It was the first shopping plaza in Elk County. The block was developed by Mylert M. Armstrong Sr. The block featured a long brick and stone structure that had retail businesses on the ground floor with residential apartments above. The Johnsonburg Post Office was formerly on the right end of the block. (Glenn Freeburg.)

This is the intersection of Market and Bridge Streets, looking up Bridge Street. On the left is the Brick Block with the Johnsonburg Post Office on the corner. In the distance is the Johnsonburg United Methodist Church at Bridge and High Streets. On the right are the Johnsonburg National Bank and right behind it, Holy Rosary Church. A lone pedestrian waits to cross a deserted intersection. (Glenn Freeburg.)

Johnsonburg residents take pride in their ability to survive and even enjoy north-central Pennsylvania winters, which can sometimes be quite northerly. Old timers scoff at each winter storm as balmy compared to storms of yore. "I remember when the drifts were so big you could hardly see over them," this gentleman could claim. (Tim Leathers.)

This beautiful brick neoclassical structure has been at the heart of Johnsonburg life since 1921, when it was built by the New York and Pennsylvania Company (the paper mill) and presented to the community. Today it is known as the Johnsonburg Community Building. It held a library, municipal offices, and meeting rooms for local organizations. It had recreational facilities and an adjacent outdoor playground.

The Town Hall connecting with the
Fire Hose Co. Dept. and Jail,
Johnsonburg, Pa.

This is the redbrick Johnsonburg City Hall at the corner of High and Spruce Streets. The building was used by many groups, including the Girl Scouts. The small, box-like Johnsonburg city jail can be seen to the right of the main building. Johnsonburg's City Hall fell into disrepair and was torn down. (Mark Wendel.)

City Jail
Johnsonburg, Pa.

Johnsonburg's old city jail appears shocking or even humorous from today's modern vantage point but it was a simpler time, a smaller community, and a slower paced world. This old-time jail looks like it could be from a western movie set. Crudely built with little ventilation, one suspects its security. Local lockups were temporary measures for less serious offenses. More serious offenders were quickly moved to the county facility. (Mark Wendel.)

In this early view of Market Street, the main byway of the town is still dirt with wooden sidewalks. There is a watering trough for horses on the right side of the street. The buildings from left to right are the Johnsonburg Press, Zierden's Department Store and the Brick Block. The building on the right side of the street is the Armstrong Opera House.

The west side of Market Street was in the heart of Johnsonburg's business district. The buildings are, from left to right, the Hyatt Pharmaceutical Company, with the Moose Club upstairs; the Elks Club; the Armstrong Opera House (later the Palace Theatre); and the Stackpole Carbon Company. The Stackpole Carbon Company building was later converted into the Johnsonburg Public Library, also housing the Johnsonburg Municipal Authority (water company), law offices, and the municipal tax office.

The Armstrong Opera House was built as the Park Opera House and Billiard Hall and was later renovated by Mylert M. Armstrong Sr. It was once billed as the finest theater between New York City and Chicago. It seated 1,000 people with a 36-foot stage and balcony. It later became a movie house known as the Palace Theatre.

Center Street in Johnsonburg is crowded with horse wagons and loitering youths with a natural curiosity for the photographer. The mansard-roofed building at the far end of the street is the Armstrong Hotel. Businesses visible are a millenary, a dentist, and a grocer with crates of produce displayed on the sidewalk. (Mark Wendel.)

Here is a good illustration of how the mill and the town always existed side by side and sometimes together. The Johnsonburg and Clermont Railroad tracks are now filled in between Center and Market Streets. The building on the left is advertising a concoction called "Duke's Mixture." There is also a barber pole in front of one of the buildings. The Sulphite Mill is at the end of the street. (Mark Wendel.)

Cobb Street, Johnsonburg, Pa.

This is a view of Cobb Street between Market and Center Streets. The Sulphite Mill towers in the background. The Johnsonburg and Clermont Railroad tracks along Market Street have since been covered. The building on the right was the freight house, and the tall building to its left is the Simchick Building, which housed the Knights of Columbus. (Mark Wendel.)

69

On Cobb Street, looking east from Center Street, the buildings are, from left to right, Bosler's Drug Store, George Limber's Pool Room, Charlie Kanski's Grocery, Jenks Family Store, the Simchick Building (later the Knights of Columbus), and the freight house (later Nelson's Store). The building on the left is advertising cigars and Coca-Cola. It is either a holiday or a lot of Johnsonburg youths are playing hooky. (Mark Wendel.)

Roy B. Constable Stores, selling furniture and housewares on Center Street in Johnsonburg, was started by the gentleman of that name in partnership with his son Melvin and Jack Rosenhoover. Roy B. Constable came to Johnsonburg from Johnstown and was active in many business ventures before founding the business that bears his name.

Here is the Ubel and Flynn Furniture and Undertaking business on Bridge Street in Johnsonburg decorated in festive bunting for some occasion. John C. Ubel Sr. came to Johnsonburg in 1889 from New York State, where his family was involved in the same businesses. Ubel later took his brother-in-law Dwight W. Flynn, a bookkeeper, and Rex Clay Loder, a relative, into the business. (Mark Wendel.)

The Ubel and Flynn Furniture and Undertaking business was operated in Johnsonburg for many years by the Ubel family and its descendants. Posing in front of the establishment in 1896 are, from left to right, Dwight W. Flynn, Ruth Ubel Winslow, John C. Ubel Sr., and Maude Ubel Walden. Winslow was one of the first female undertakers in Pennsylvania when both undertaking and business were considered inappropriate for women. (Mark Wendel.)

Bridge Street looking North.
Johnsonburg, Pa.

This scene is looking north, across Bridge Street and up First Avenue. Spruce Street can be seen crossing the next block. The Avenues area is still mostly undeveloped with few houses. Today Avenue Hill is filled with residences. It is a good bet that the photographer's automobile is parked in the foreground. What he or she was documenting is unknown. (Mark Wendel.)

Ted Wilhelm Sr. and Harry Mann founded Wilmann Pontiac after World War II, and it is still family-owned in West Johnsonburg. The family resided in the apartments above the business. It looks much the same today, although the gasoline pumps have been removed. The light towers of Johnsonburg Memorial Field can be seen in the right background.

The New Armstrong Hotel is shown here on Bridge Street in Johnsonburg. The Armstrong Hotel was a world-class establishment at one time featuring 60 rooms. The large dining room served the finest cuisine, and the hotel offered many other amenities. In 1908, the business became the New Armstrong and then the Straessley and in the 1930s, suffered a major fire and was torn down. (Mark Wendel.)

The Hotel Johnsonburg was a four-story, brick structure that offered 30 rooms at $2 per day. It had an elegant dining room and handsome bar. The hotel was built around a mineral well that served the guests, some claiming with beneficial results. Famous heavyweight boxing champion John L. Sullivan, who had relatives in Johnsonburg, lived here while training for fights. Note the stepping-stone in front of the building. (Mark Wendel.)

S. R. Armstrong's Residence, Johnsonburg, Pa.

This is Chestnut Street at Penn Avenue. The elegant Queen Anne–style mansion on the left is the residence of Samuel R. Armstrong, the manager of the paper mill. The building later became the Penn Club. Today it houses the Ferragine Funeral Home. Further up Chestnut Street is St. Martin's Episcopal Church, which burned, and behind that is the Johnsonburg High School on Second Avenue, which was torn down. (Glenn Freeburg.)

First Ave. Looking North, Johnsonburg, Pa.

This is the intersection of First Avenue and Chestnut Street looking down First Avenue. The mansion in the center was the residence of paper mill manager Samuel R. Armstrong. Avenue Hill was a prime residential neighborhood. Note the abundance of trees planted along the dirt roads. Also note the windmill in the distance above the house on the right-center. (Mark Wendel.)

Another view of the intersection of First Avenue and Chestnut Street is shown looking down First. The Armstrong House is on the left, and St. Martin's Episcopal Church, which burned, is on the right. In the distance, down First Avenue, the steeple of the First Baptist Church on the right and the tower of the 1896 wood frame school on the left are visible. (Mark Wendel.)

This Tudor-style residence is one of the stateliest mansions in Johnsonburg and is located on Penn Avenue at Chestnut Street. The house was built for mill official E. L. Myers and later occupied by Neal Jones, superintendent of the paper mill. His two daughters are on the steps. Note the attractive landscaping and the extensive garden on the right. A groundskeeper can be seen at work, also at right. (Mark Wendel.)

75

Bridge St., East of Penn St., Johnsonburg, Pa.

This is the intersection of Bridge Street and High Street. High Street can be seen intersecting with Penn Street in the background. The building on the corner was the Nolan Boarding Home for many years. Just visible in the left foreground are the steps of the First Methodist Episcopal Church, since burned. Holy Rosary Church is just out of the photograph to the right. (Mark Wendel.)

First Avenue, Johnsonburg, Pa.

This photograph shows how grand some of the residential streets of Johnsonburg were when they were new and properly landscaped. It invites the shade-loving stroller. This sylvan, tree-lined avenue is First Avenue with Bridge Street crossing in the foreground. The streets are dirt, and the sidewalks are wooden. These lovely homes originally housed mill officials. (Mark Wendel.)

Here is a scene from the laying of the cornerstone of Holy Rosary Church in Johnsonburg at the corner of Bridge and Penn Streets on July 17, 1904, under the direction of Bishop John Fitzmaurice of Erie. Penn Street is seen winding its way up the hill in the background. (Mark Wendel.)

Here is the completed structure of Holy Rosary Church. The view is looking up Penn Street. The church was dedicated in 1906. This brick building replaced an earlier wood frame church at the corner of Market and Spruce Streets, built in 1889. Before 1876, Johnsonburg Catholics traveled to Kane for services until residents organized a local parish. (Mark Wendel.)

Presbyterian Church,
Johnsonburg, Pa.

The First Presbyterian Church in Johnsonburg stood on the corner of Bridge Street and Second Avenue and was built in 1892. On December 26, 1948, the church was destroyed by fire while Sunday school was underway. The church was rebuilt from the ruins but is no longer standing. In 1967, the First Presbyterian Church was united with the Methodist churches of Johnsonburg. (Mark Wendel.)

High Street, Johnsonburg, Pa.

Methodism started in Johnsonburg in 1888 at Rolfe. A group of worshippers left to worship in places in Johnsonburg before deciding that they needed a structure of their own in which to worship. This big redbrick church at the corner of Bridge and High Streets was built in 1900. After it burned, many of the members and church furnishings moved back to the United Methodist Church in Rolfe. (Mark Wendel.)

St. John's Evangelical Lutheran Church was built in 1900 on a plot of ground in West Johnsonburg that was donated by the Kistler Tanning Company. Prior to the erection of this building, the congregation met in the Methodist church in Rolfe since its inception in 1888. Original services were conducted in German.

High School, Johnsonburg, Pa.

The first Johnsonburg High School was built at the top of the hill on Second Avenue in 1894. The redbrick structure was four stories tall, counting the foundation level. It originally had eight large rooms. In 1918, after being abandoned, it was deemed unsafe as plaster was beginning to fall, and the building was torn down. (Mark Wendel.)

The Rolfe School is shown here in 1906. The time must be recess, as most students are out on the lawn playing while a few look on from upstairs windows. This school had a line drawn down the middle to demarcate the sections; one side was for students from Rolfe, and the other was for students from the west end of Johnsonburg. Note the old-fashioned bell cupola and outhouse behind the building.

In 1915, this redbrick school was built at First Avenue and Spruce Street replacing the wooden building, visible at left, with grade school on the first floor, high school on the second floor, and a gymnasium in the basement. A buff brick high school was built on the lot at left, connected to this building by a bridge. Both buildings were removed for modern replacements in 1964 and 1971. (Glenn Freeburg.)

In 1922, the Holy Rosary School was built on Market Street in Johnsonburg. It was staffed by Sisters of St. Joseph from their motherhouse in Erie. The school closed its doors in 1962 when Catholic schools were consolidated in the county at Elk County Christian High School in St. Marys. (Mark Wendel.)

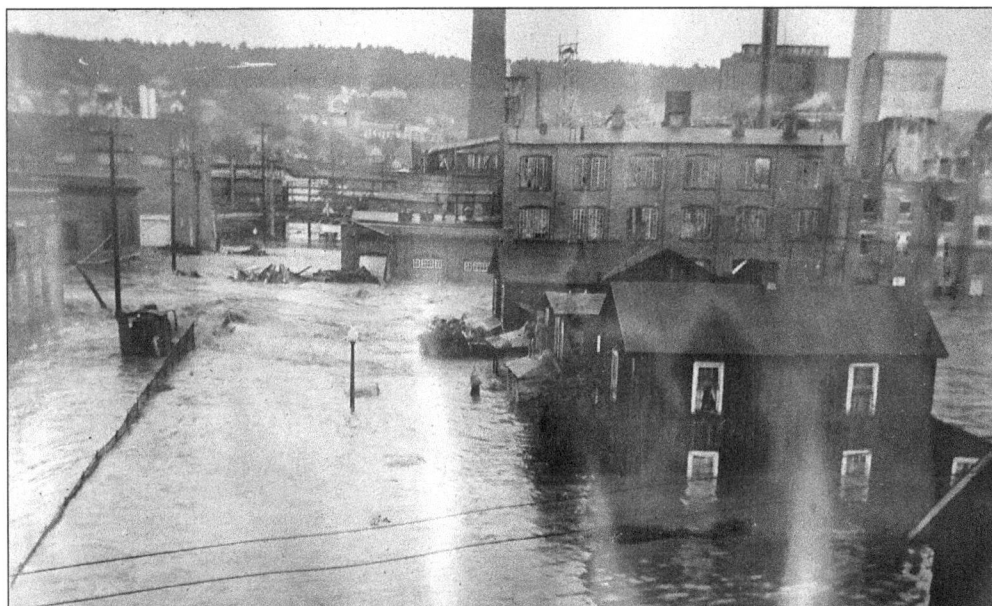

This scene is from the flood of 1942 along Center Street. The main office of the paper mill is visible on the left of the photograph. Two people are standing in knee-deep water talking to two people stranded on a porch roof in the Tannery Row section of Johnsonburg. Several people had to be rescued from the high water.

On July 17 and 18, 1942, one of the most intense thunderstorms ever to be recorded in the United States hit north-central Pennsylvania with torrential rain. At Instanter, upriver from Johnsonburg, 18.5 inches fell in 18 hours. Located at the juncture of the two branches of the Clarion River, Johnsonburg has suffered through many severe floods over the years, but this storm resulted in the worst flooding in Johnsonburg's history.

The great flood of 1942 caused extensive property damage in Johnsonburg as can be witnessed in this photograph. Houses seem to be behaving like dominoes and all falling down in a row. Such is the awesome power of water and man's ineffective attempt to control it. Of the 24 homes in the Clarion Junction area, only 5 were left standing on their foundations after the waters had done their work.

Johnsonburg is located at the juncture of the two branches of the Clarion River and was often devastated by major flooding. The situation was not alleviated until the construction of the East Branch Reservoir in the early 1950s. These homes were knocked off their foundations from rising floodwaters from the flood of 1942.

Johnsonburg was a major rail junction in 1942, when the great flood devastated the community and rail connections. The Pennsylvania Railroad, the B&O, the Erie Railroad, and the paper mill lines all traversed the town. Some 20 boxcars were lost and several bridges. However, all of the businesses rebuilt quickly. This scene is typical of the close proximity of housing and rail lines in Johnsonburg.

This scene is from the 1942 flood and depicts the area of Cobb Street between Center and Market Streets. The paper mill's Sulphite Mill rises up in the left background. In front of that is Rosenhoover Brother's Billiards, a Cash and Carry business, the Kendall station, and across the street, Bosler's Drug Store, George Limber's Pool Hall, Charlie Kanski's Grocery Store, and the Jenks Family Store. (Steve Michuck.)

Center Street in Johnsonburg shows, from left to right, Eagen's Hardware selling Kemtone paint, Dave Friedman's Clothing and Shoe Store, and the Rosenhoover Brother's Billiards. The men are cleaning up after a flood. Note the high water mark on the windows. Johnsonburg was often down but never out. The New York and Pennsylvania Company's Sulphite Mill looms in the right background. There was no separation between mill and town.

The great flood of 1942 claimed eight automobiles. These three vehicles behind the Kendall filling station on Center Street were jammed together and then debris was stacked up against them by the surging waters. Not as many people owned cars back then, and it was a major investment. Not as many people had insurance either.

The Pennsylvania Railroad's trestle at the juncture of the Clarion River branches is lying on its side, taken out by the flood of 1942. The East Branch is to the left and the West Branch is to the right, appearing as one body of water. At the top right is the Flats area of Johnsonburg between the Pennsylvania Railroad tracks and the Clarion River. That lively section of Johnsonburg was wiped out by the flood and not rebuilt.

Here is the scene on Grant Street after the 1942 flood. This area was known as the Flats south and west of the mill, and it never recovered from this flood. The area is empty today. Most of this debris was removed by hand as there was no heavy equipment available. These spectators survey the damage in front of Joe Marrone's Grocery Store. (Steve Michuck.)

The paper mill creates an impressive, almost overpowering backdrop to the Grant Street Baseball Grounds in Johnsonburg. The imposing behemoth, the smokestacks, and the smell of sulfur must have given the local nine a distinct home field advantage. Small towns competed intensely with other towns for athletic superiority, and athletes often became legendary local heroes. (Mark Wendel.)

Four

JONES TOWNSHIP

This is the beautiful valley originally named Buena Vista and now called Wilcox. Today it is a peaceful village located on the West Branch of the Clarion River but in times past it once had the largest tannery in the world, which can be seen on the left of this photograph. The Wilcox School building is prominent in the foreground.

The Crocker blacksmith shop in Wilcox is pictured. Before the age of automobiles, keeping horses and wagons of all sorts functioning was a necessity, and the village blacksmith was essential to any community. Many enjoy watching other people work, whether it is a car, a horse, or a photographer, as this gang of interested observers attests. Blacksmith John Lindberg is fourth from the right in the white shirt.

This is the J. L. Brown Banking Company in Wilcox. In 1926, the business became the Wilcox National Bank. In 1931, during the Depression, the bank closed. It is decorated here in festive bunting for some holiday occasion. The building was later occupied by the post office, a grocery/meat store, and library. Today the building is owned by the Mason's Lodge.

This is the Spettique Building at the corner of Oak and Marvin Streets in Wilcox. It is a time of dirt streets and wooden sidewalks. The upstairs of the Spettique Building housed the Wilcox Social Club, which had card tables, pool tables, and a reading room. The clubhouse seems to be a focal point of socializing in front of the building also.

Here is an interior view of the Wilcox Social Club in 1915. This gathering place was located in the upstairs of the Spettique Building in Wilcox. Besides pool tables, the club also featured tables for playing cards and a small collection of books. These inviting rooms were tastefully furnished with framed scenes on the walls and fashionable drapes. Note the old-fashioned gaslights.

The Smith Brothers Company was a general merchandise store located on Marvin Street in Wilcox. The first store on the site, the Town and Country Store, was built by Alonzo I. Wilcox and Lucius Wilcox. When that store burned, the Company Store was erected and was later purchased by the Smith Brothers Company of Ridgway.

Dutch's Freezette was a dairy and lunch counter located on the Johnsonburg–Wilcox Road, Route 219. The building is still there although in disrepair, its time gone. The business was replaced by the even faster corporate food chains that sprang up like mushrooms throughout America. The bare bones of the structure remind travelers of the rural roadside of a bygone America.

The Wilcox House was the first hotel in Wilcox and was opened by Thomas J. Goodwin. An interesting fact about this hotel is that one of the hotel's registers reveals that Jefferson Davis, president of the Confederacy, was once registered there, and the hotel was the site where Gen. Thomas L. Kane registered volunteers for his famed Bucktail Regiment to fight against the Confederacy. Pres. Ulysses S. Grant also visited here.

Col. Alonzo I. Wilcox began his fortune in the lumbering business in Wilcox. In 1861, he lost his sawmill and $100,000 worth of lumber in a flood. Wilcox then went into railroading and oil interests and recovered his losses. He represented the area in the state legislature. After his wife died, he moved his family to Bradford. His home, shown here, is now used as the American Legion clubhouse.

The McFarland House hotel in Wilcox is in business at the juncture of Wilson Run and the West Branch of the Clarion River. The building has been restored and is a popular spot with fishermen and travelers. This group enjoying a summer day includes several men with shovels, possibly road workers.

The Grant House in Wilcox was built in 1882 and named for Ulysses S. Grant, who visited the village twice to fish with his friends Thomas L. Kane and Alonzo I. Wilcox. Grant never stayed here. It was built after his visits. On this day, proprietor J. O'Leary has a large well-dressed clientele for some unknown occasion.

The Nazareth Evangelical Lutheran Church, left, and its parsonage, right, in Wilcox are pictured in this scene with two men lounging under a lamppost. The first Lutheran services in Wilcox were held in the public school buildings under the direction of pastors from Kane in 1875. They built their own building in 1881, and the parsonage followed in 1901. Until the mid-20th century, services were in Swedish. (Glenn Freeburg.)

The first Catholic families in Wilcox traveled to Kane for services before erecting their own place of worship. This is the first Catholic church in Wilcox; it was a wood frame structure built in 1889 when the parish numbered 25 families. This church burned to the ground in 1949 and was replaced by a new building, St. Anne's Catholic Church of Wilcox. (Glenn Freeburg.)

Today the Wilcox School District has been combined with the Johnsonburg School District, but in the past, Wilcox had its own schools. Four of the buildings stood on this site. The first school was a wood frame building and later ones were brick. At times, it was a grade school or high school and sometimes both. The final school building has been converted into a community building and park. (Glenn Freeburg.)

There is much conjecture about where the first school in Jones Township was located. It was probably in the northern half of the township when that area was part of McKean County, making it the first school in what was to become Elk County. Those scholars got to their studies in this horse-drawn wagon in the 1920s and 1930s, bumping over primitive roads in all kinds of weather.

The Wilcox sawmill was owned by Henry, Bayard and Company of Philadelphia and built around 1870. It was later leased by John Ernhout. Note the long wooden covered bridge of the Philadelphia and Erie (later Pennsylvania) Railroad in the foreground. This mill sawed the lumber generated by timber cut for the Wilcox Tannery, the largest in the world at one time.

The Wilcox Tannery was reportedly the largest in the world at one time. John Ernhout and Maurice Schultz organized the operation. Hemlock bark for the complex was cut by Henry, Bayard and Company of Philadelphia in Jones Township and McKean County. Several sawmills were needed to keep up with the tannery's needs. After several mergers, declining business, and the gutting of the buildings, the great tannery burned in 1966.

This is the Wilcox Window Glass Company's plant in Wilcox. This location is where the old road to Kane, presently State Route 321 meets Burning Well and Horner Roads. Herman Swanson's house is at the left. Wilcox is located where Wilson Run joins the West Branch of the Clarion River and in its early days had several diverse industries such as this one.

This photograph shows the Pennsylvania Railroad's freight station on the left and passenger station on the right in Wilcox. Several employees are awaiting the arrival of the next train with their handcart to unload baggage. Note the fancy roof brackets on the passenger terminal. The Pennsylvania Railroad always tried to add a touch of class to the architecture of its buildings. Both structures have since fallen to the wrecking ball.

When the big woods were being cut in north-central Pennsylvania, sawmills were everywhere. Sawmills used holding ponds to move logs around the operation. The ruins of these dams are still discernible in many places in the area today. The ruins of the old milldam in Wilcox are a playground for these boys getting a view from the bridge over Wilson Run.

Rock Run Bridge, Wilcox, Pa.

A white horse–drawn surrey has paused on the Rocky Run Bridge in Wilcox to be entertained by a trio of minstrels with dog and accordion. This idyllic, sylvan scene leaves much to the imagination. Who is in the carriage? Who is taking the photograph? Were rural serenades common? A picture is worth a thousand words and leaves a thousand questions.

The swinging bridge over the West Branch of the Clarion River was a curiosity in Wilcox and often portrayed on postcards. The West Branch is a sizable watercourse when it is full, and those living on the other side of the road needed access to their homes. Here a solitary gentleman contemplates his reflection and the magic and mystery of flowing water.

The swinging bridge in Wilcox was solidly constructed and was a fixture on the West Branch for years. It could support one or it could host a party, as seems to be going on here for some unknown reason. Everyone in the area apparently had dressed in their best suits and bowler hats to stand on the bridge for a photograph.

The Joy Garden's Dining and Dancing Club was located on Route 219 between Wilcox and Johnsonburg. It was a popular nightspot featuring local and area live music for many years. After its years as a nightclub, the spacious interior became a roller-skating rink. Roller-skating was quite popular in the past and most towns of any size boasted of a rink. (Thomas Folino.)

Twin Lakes is a recreational facility within the Allegheny National Forest north of Wilcox. There is a large bathhouse and swimming facilities. The lake had a sand beach and at one time had a diving dock offshore. The site was originally owned by the McKean Chemical Company, which made wood alcohol from the surrounding woodlands. A splash dam provided water to the business, which closed in the 1920s. (Mark Wendel.)

Bendigo State Park was developed because the children of Johnsonburg needed a place to swim in the summertime. A park was developed in the 1920s at an old abandoned lumber town on the East Branch of the Clarion River. In 1936, the Works Progress Administration built a small dam to form a pool. This dam survived the flood of 1942. Today the area has a modern swimming pool. (Author's collection.)

Instanter was a logging community on the upper East Branch of the Clarion River. In the early 1950s, when the East Branch Dam was filled, Instanter disappeared under the waters of the new lake but not forever. Instanter was located at the very end of the new impoundment, and whenever there are drought conditions, the site of Instanter is once again above water, and former residents sometimes stage a reunion.

Instanter was a company town, built in 1889 around a new branch of the Wilcox Tannery. Henry Schimmelfeng also constructed a sawmill, and the village was served by the new Johnsonburg and Clermont Railroad. Tenant houses were built, and an active village life developed until business declined, the tannery closed, and finally, the town was buried beneath the waters of the East Branch Dam in the early 1950s.

Instanter possessed all of the amenities of any town, including general stores, a post office, churches, schools, rooming houses, and taverns. Instanter even had a summer camp with tennis courts and a swimming pool. It had a well-maintained baseball diamond, and its hometown nine were often champions of the area. The region was also a noted mecca for sportsmen, with hunting and fishing being popular activities.

101

Instanter was a vibrant little community for a while in the first half of the 20th century. The tannery and sawmill were surrounded by a seemingly inexhaustible supply of natural resources. But as always, when the environment is taken for granted, time steals prosperity, and eventually the businesses ran out of trees to profit from. The mills closed, and the waters swirled over the vanished golden age of unbroken forest.

The tannery at Instanter was built by the Schultz family, who owned the largest tannery in the world at Wilcox. It was built in 1890, one of the last tanneries to be built in Pennsylvania. Recently many tourists visited the site of Instanter, which today is Elk State Park, when the water level of East Branch Dam was lowered for repairs and remnants of the bygone town emerged from the mud.

Instanter was located on the upper East Branch of the Clarion River. This bridge scene is from 1907. In 2007, drought conditions in the area caused the East Branch Dam's water level to decline and remnants of the town emerged from the mud at the end of the impoundment. In 2008, when engineers lowered the dam for inspection, the site of Instanter became a tourist attraction once again.

In 2008, seepage at the East Branch Dam caused fears about the dam's safety, and the reservoir was drawn down to the lowest levels since it was built in 1952. Many tourists ventured to the dam's upper end to see the remains of the former town of Instanter rise out of the mud. Not much is left to witness except the foundations of former buildings and some bridge abutments. (Author's collection.)

Straight was a lumbering community on the Clarion River at Straight Creek that today is under the waters of East Branch Dam. The site originally had a log cabin that was used by Pres. Ulysses S. Grant as a fishing camp. Note the lush gardens that are fenced in to keep out livestock.

Upland was a famous stagecoach and wagon stop on the Milesburg–Smethport Turnpike located on the Elk–McKean County border. W. P. Wilcox built his home here in 1842. He later sold the building to Thomas L. Kane, the founder of Kane and organizer of the famous and decorated Bucktail Regiment, when Kane married in 1857. Famous visitors to the residence include Ulysses S. Grant, Simon Cameron, and Theodore Roosevelt.

On August 5, 1906, the Straight sawmill burned with a pond full of logs and two years of cutting left on the tract. The town of Straight was built by Martin F. Quinn and included a sawmill and chemical plant. The decision was made to construct a new mill to finish the tract. Straight eventually became a ghost town before the site was flooded by the East Branch Dam.

The former Glen Hazel schoolhouse, now the Riverside Lodge, is located on the East Branch of the Clarion River. The Riverside Lodge suffered damage and the bridge was washed away by the monumental storm and flash flood that inundated the region in July 1942. There is a large stone beside the Riverside Lodge marking the purchase of the first state game lands in Pennsylvania by the Pennsylvania Game Commission. (Steve Michuck.)

Ground has been cleared and the breast of the East Branch Dam is taking shape with the help of giant earthmovers and the dwarfed workers of this huge project. The dam cost $9 million, covers 1,370 acres, and is 6.2 miles long. It holds 30.6 billion gallons of water, which in 1954 could supply the entire country with water for four hours or Johnsonburg for 83 years.

Workers are putting the finishing touches on the breast of East Branch Dam. In 2008, seeps in the breast of the dam caused concerns, and the dam was drawn down for testing by the Army Corps of Engineers. Water levels were at their lowest levels since the structure was built. The ruins of Instanter a town at the dam's upper end, which was flooded, were once again visible.

Here is a view of the spillway of East Branch Dam under construction. The device is a deep trench and dwarfs the large cranes being used to build the structure. Note there is a truck in the trench at the far end. There is also a long wooden stairway for workers to go down in the hole, and there are wooden forms built to pour concrete into.

The completed spillway is a long, deep concrete trench used to release water during high water and has only been used once, in June 1972, during Hurricane Agnes. Emergency rescue workers have used the site to practice rescue techniques during a disaster. Deer have also fallen into the spillway and have been rescued by the game commission.

Construction was started on the East Branch Dam in 1947 after disastrous flooding in western Pennsylvania in 1936 and 1942. The United States Army Corps of Engineers built a series of dams to protect the watershed. In this scene, the control tower is nearing completion in 1951. This structure is actually the tallest structure in Elk County, although two-thirds of it is underwater.

In the early 1950s, the East Branch Dam was completed and ready to be filled. It became operational in December 1952. Surrounded by state forest, state game lands, and state parkland, the area has become the recreational magnet for Elk County. The first state game lands purchased in Pennsylvania were just downstream of the dam. Elk State Park is located at the upper end of the reservoir today. (Mark Wendel.)

This is a view of the East Branch Dam on the Clarion River, shortly after it was finished 7.3 miles upstream from Johnsonburg. Built for flood control purposes in western Pennsylvania and Pittsburgh, Johnsonburg was the closest beneficiary. Floods had devastated the community in 1936 and 1942. As the dam was being filled in 1952, it prevented another major flood.

Here is another photograph taken by the Army Corps of Engineers to record the finished project. This view is across the breast of the dam to the spillway. Water went over the spillway only one time in the dam's history, during June 1972, when Hurricane Agnes dumped massive amounts of rain on New York and Pennsylvania.

Here is a view of the East Branch Dam shortly after its completion. The dam was dedicated on August 8, 1954. Boat races were held for the occasion in front of a group of dignitaries including both state senators Edward Martin and James Duff, also both former governors of the state. This view is looking across the spillway toward the control tower side of the impoundment.

The lessons of the failure of Ketner Dam in 1911 at Glen Hazel, seven miles above Johnsonburg, were unheeded at the Austin Dam only 35 miles away. Johnsonburg was flooded, but nobody died; 78 people at Austin, however, paid for the miscalculation with their lives just one month later. Both were just-completed concrete structures and were overcome by heavy rains. Austin gained worldwide fame while Ketner Dam sleeps on in this little remembered corner of Elk County. (John Fedorko.)

Five

COMMUNITY

It is unknown whether this is a Fourth of July, a Memorial Day, or a Veterans Day parade coming up Bridge Street. All serve as valuable civics lessons to teach the young the values of this country's way of life. Amid the profusion of Old Glories, several of the boys are wearing military uniforms, including a sailor suit. One of the children carries a (hopefully) toy gun.

Italian Catholic immigrants who religiously preserved their customs with great pride settled Johnsonburg. Passing on their way of life to the next generation was important to them, including their joy of life and love of music. Work was strenuous and serious and so was celebrating. Holidays, feast days, weddings, and anniversaries were numerous, and all needed music to enliven the merriment.

The International Order of Odd Fellows parade marches up Bridge Street past the bank and Holy Rosary Church in Johnsonburg on April 26, 1912. The Odd Fellows were known for their parades and marching bands, and there seems to be a large crowd in the distance at the intersection of Bridge and Market Streets enjoying the spectacle. (Mark Wendel.)

The Five Aces Orchestra was led by Bleach Perantoni (left). Live music was always popular and every town had local favorite amateur and semiamateur ensembles. For every amateur musician who became famous thousands played in obscurity just for the love of their music. Note the phone number only has four numbers. (Mark Wendel.)

THE FIVE ACES ORCHESTRA
BLEACH   JOHNNY   RUDY   BILL   JIM

DANCES   FLOOR SHOWS   BANQUETS

CALL OR WRITE BLEACH PERANTONI, 513 Third Ave., Johnsonburg, Pa., Ph. 5304

The Armstrong Yellow Jackets Bugle Corps was a precision marching band that performed in shows and competitions around the region. The unit won many trophies for its talents and was a pride of the community. They were an imposing sight strutting down the midway in full voice in their snappy yellow and black uniforms. Here they are seen in one of the area towns pleasing the crowds.

113

Children in any age were a precious commodity, and doting parents always wanted a keepsake photograph to fondly look back on in future years. One can only assume there is just such a precious child somewhere under the giant ball of feathers and bonnet in this old-time sled. The brave, cherubic face peering out from this bundle of fluff can be excused for appearing slightly overwhelmed.

Children can be amazingly creative. Hitching the family pooches to a wagon makes a dandy pretend horse and buggy for one whose full-time job is playing. This cowboy-in-training (before electronic toys) is headed west, at least to the end of the yard. Dressing up in a period costume brings the Wild West home for this child in the Glen Hazel area.

A man teaches his grandson about the wide world of the background garden dressed in the fashion of the day for young and old including straw hats. Passing on family values and generational advice is an extended family affair. Johnsonburg is known for strong family ties and large families that support and encourage each other.

Here is a photograph of a photographer. A man and his children pose for a photograph at a log cabin retreat in the forests of Elk County. Many area residents enjoyed the outdoor life by building cabins out in the woods to escape the bustle of town life. This well-dressed gentleman appears to be a photographer himself judging by the equipment he is holding.

Five stylish young girlfriends, one of them wearing bloomers, pose on a bridge. On a hot summer day when swimming is not an option, just peacefully watching a cold, gurgling mountain stream has a cooling effect that helps one get through the rest of the day. Running water has a magnetism that soothes the spirit. This scene is from the Tambine area between Wilcox and Johnsonburg.

Fashions change but not the irresistible urge to get ones portrait taken in the latest style to remember just how debonair one was. Millinery shops are uncommon today but were very popular back when hats were the essential topper for a woman's wardrobe. Promenading about town to show off the latest designer bonnet was a social ritual and made many a conquest.

At one time, Johnsonburg was a much busier place than it is today. It boasted of several restaurants including the Johnsonburg Restaurant that was open 24 hours a day. Many restaurants had counters at which ladies were not allowed to sit, it being deemed unladylike. These two elegantly dressed Johnsonburg lasses are nothing if not ladylike. (Glenn Freeburg.)

The Johnsonburg High School's graduating class numbered a sparse four scholars in 1907. Schools had far fewer students in times past not just because the population was smaller. Today advanced schooling is essential, unlike the past when laboring jobs were readily available in a blue-collar town like Johnsonburg. The bright spot was that one could unabashedly tell prospective employers that they had finished fourth in their class. (Mark Wendel.)

Before everything was machine-made and mass-produced, rural settlements often hand produced what they needed. Farmers were especially inventive in fashioning their own clothing, tools, machinery, everyday necessities, and even vehicles. This simple, crudely built donkey cart is ready to attend to the day's chores overseen by the faithful pet dog.

A gentleman has dressed up in his best suit, bow tie, and straw hat to get a studio portrait taken with possibly two of his favorite things, man's best friend and a cold brew. People grow attached to their pets, so why not have a photograph taken to remember the faithful companion when he has been replaced by a new best friend.

This early type of bicycle used to be known as a "bonecrusher" because they had no suspension and really rattled the teeth. When bicycles were first invented, clubs formed to ride the machines and aficionados were known as wheelmen. Radical changes to the design of the vehicle made them even more popular.

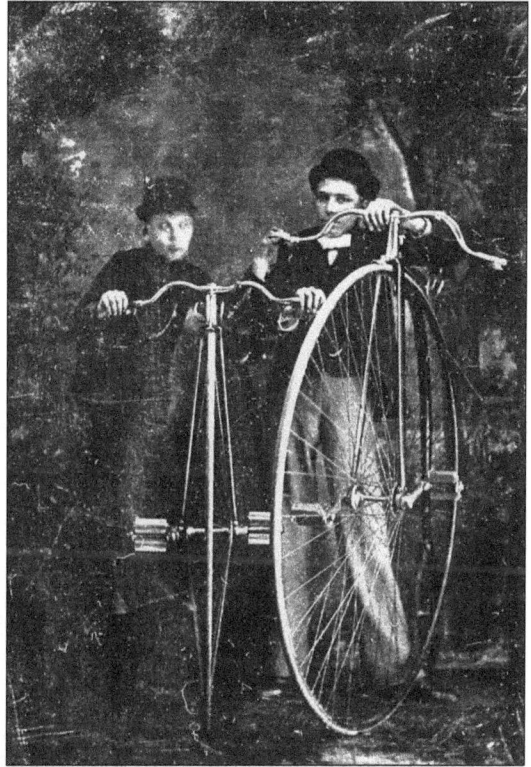

The strength of any area is not in the people who exploited the resources and moved on but in those who stayed. People who believed that a place was good to labor in for a lifetime, raise a house and family, teach their heirs the same values, and continue their legacy are the true lifeblood of a community. Honor and respect are due those who have come before and smoothed the path.

People loved to have their portrait taken in a studio and were often creative in their dress or staging. Showing off a leisure activity or hobby for the camera told the viewer that the subject was competent at their chosen avocation. It is unknown whether this roller-skater was adept at that sport, but it can be said that he was flamboyant and well dressed. (Glenn Freeburg.)

Two comrades in arms pose for a photograph to demonstrate their unswerving loyalty and fraternity in front of the Clarion Hotel in the middle of Center Street in Johnsonburg. If they are lucky, all of the traffic will avoid them as the automobile on the left is. Note the smokestacks of the mill in the left background. Perhaps they have just finished their shift and have stopped for liquid refreshment.

Men's social clubs were always popular. Some had elaborate rituals and customs running the gamut from solemn to whimsical. Enjoying a beverage with friends was the basis for many of these organizations. These clubmen have dressed up for a studio portrait of their group. Note that the aim of the man pouring from the jug is slightly off. He is missing his friend's goblet.

Hiking through the woods and picnicking were popular activities for both genders in past times when there were far fewer diversions than today. These wayfarers are often portrayed in their best clothes, possibly because after church on Sunday was the best time for a leisurely stroll. Waterfalls, rock formations, and commercial picnic groves were popular destinations for these ventures.

The Decker Memorial Fountain on East Center Street in Johnsonburg honors native son Horace Alvin Decker, who was killed at Le Cheve Tondu, France, in 1918 during World War I. His remains were returned home and were buried in 1921. Johnsonburg is extremely proud of its citizens who fight and sometimes die in defense of their way of life in all just battles, including current conflicts. (Mark Wendel.)

Johnsonburg has always been proud of its contribution to the defense of this country in times of trouble. This is the welcome home celebration on September 2, 1946, parading on Market Street in front of Holy Rosary School. This is just the naval contingent. Johnsonburg supplied many heroes to this great cause. Note the Straub beer truck refreshing parade watchers at the left with this Elk County product.

Johnsonburg has just cause to be proud of its reliant and dedicated fire department. They have upgraded their equipment to become a modern, efficient service. Here is the Armstrong Hose Company's first fire truck pumper. The building in the background is the former Geary home, which was later the Holy Rosary Rectory and the American Legion.

One of the popular recreational activities around the area is four wheeling. Testing one's driving skill and their vehicle's stamina on back roads, trails, paths, snow, swamps, and even streams entertains many outdoor enthusiasts. Getting a vehicle unstuck is as much fun as getting it stuck in the first place. Elk County is the perfect backdrop for commercials for off-road vehicles. The merits of one vehicle or another makes for interesting campfire debate.

The first visitors to the Elk County region were hunters and trappers. The first settlers also supplemented their farming with wild game. Hunting is still a popular avocation for area residents even in the winter. The snows in the area are often deep, and snowshoes come in handy for getting around the woods.

Elk County lies in the heart of the Pennsylvania Wilds Heritage Region and the Allegheny National Forest. Hunting has been a way of life for the people of the area since the first settlers came to this forested wilderness. Children learn the mysteries of the outdoors and gun safety at the knees of their fathers and grandfathers, even little girls.

The best playground for young men is the great outdoors. From the look on these young nimrod's faces, it is apparent that they take their sport seriously. Coon hunting involves racing through the woods at night chasing the sound of the hounds through the rugged hollows of Elk County. Although these mongrels do not appear to be of the pedigreed variety, they are obviously successful nonetheless.

Hunting for rabbits is a popular sport in the Johnsonburg area, and Rolfe has a beagle club to promote the bloodlines and raising of that breed known as the best rabbit dogs. These sportsmen and their beagles are hunting from the Depression camp in the Glen Hazel area. From their catch, it is apparent that the white snowshoe hares as well as brown cottontail rabbits abound in the area.

Johnsonburg has always been a fisherman's paradise. The East and West Branches of the Clarion River as well as many tributary streams afford the happy angler ample opportunity to bend his rod in pursuit of the finned trophies. The first day of trout season in April is a time-honored custom and area holiday for locals and visitors alike.

The smaller the boy, the smaller the fish needs to be to make the beginning angler swell with pride at his accomplishment and pose for a photograph opportunity to record the moment for posterity. This one may never have been mounted on a wall, but the East Branch Dam has yielded up many a trophy to the knowledgeable sportsman or woman that knows where to dangle their worm.

Rural humor postcards often depict scenes such as this; however it actually does happen during deer season when so many hunters are chasing deer around the woods. Deer such as this trophy buck may pop up just about anywhere. Many a seasoned hunter has been sitting on the camp porch after a fruitless day afield when the big one lopes through the yard. (Glenn Freeburg.)

Music once rang out from the isolated logging boomtown of Instanter. Music dulled the loneliness of a primitive frontier. The ethnic immigrant populations of these forest-clearing patches were fiercely patriotic, and Old Glory was serenaded on this Independence Day concert. Today, amid muddy foundations of ghost buildings of the past, folk music sings out once again from nostalgic visitors and descendants, trying to commune with a lost town's vanished folk.

Visit us at
arcadiapublishing.com

www.ingramcontent.com/pod-product-compliance
Lightning Source LLC
Chambersburg PA
CBHW050641110426
42813CB00007B/1879